Complications of Having Feet

Raymond

Bizzari

Clare Songbirds Publishing House Poetry Series
ISBN 978-1-947653-88-7
Clare Songbirds Publishing House
Complications of Having Feet © 2020 Ray Bizzari

Printed in the United States of America
FIRST EDITION

Clare Songbirds Publishing House Mission Statement:
Clare Songbirds Publishing House was established to provide
a print forum for the creation of limited edition, fine art from
poets and writers, both established and emerging. We strive to
reignite and continue a tradition of quality, accessible literary
arts to the national and international community of writers, and
readers. Chapbook manuscripts are carefully chosen for their
ability to propel the expansion of art and ideas in literary form.
We provide an accessible way to promote the art of words in
order to resonate with, and impact, readers not yet familiar with
the siren song of poets and writers. Clare Songbirds Publishing
House espouses a singular cultural development where poetry
creates community and becomes commonplace in public places.

140 Cottage Street
Auburn, New York 13021
www.claresongbirdspub.com

Contents

Cairns	6
Fins	9
Hiatus	10
Opinions	11
Because	12
Rheumy	14
Norelco	15
Bye	16
DNR	17
Decline	18
Wakes	21
Skin	23
Seance	26
Insomnia	28
slick	29
Query	30
Amends	31

"Fins" first appeared in *The Comstock Review*
Fall/Winter 2016 Edition

*per la mia
famiglia
specialmente per
quelli che
sono andati
avanti*

cairns

I know a place
way up a stream
where roiling water
carved a glen,
eons of
shale work

there's a run
between
the first waterfall
up from the lake
and the next rush
further upstream
that winds through a purple
shade where green mossy
rocks, cracked and cracked again
by the sinewy, spidery roots
of tall, straight trunked trees
soar to a vertigo sky

someone piled cairns there,
using carefully selected
stones,
glacier ground,
cold water polished
stones
spaced across
the smooth,
shiny wet slate
stream bed,
magic islands dotting
the midstream rapids
in this fairy tale
forest

it's the same water
gushing thru that cut
for most of forever,
hauling silt to

where the waters
mix up a fecund
mush where
fishes go to spray their roe,
and one day,
some adventurous fish
surfaced to waddle
up the bank
where a younger sun
dried her gills
into primitive lungs

the fishes rejoiced
at this hard won
freedom
and grew legs
and arms
to celebrate,
not knowing then
because knowing
came later,
that they
traded one form
of detention
for another

Image by Brittywing

Fins

Sitting on a dock
in an end of summer wind
I drift to the voices
belonging to the couple
across the lake and
try to make them out,
their argument
chasing across
the water
banging into the pilings
making vibrations
on my sandals.

Somewhere inside a house
on this shoreline,
a woman starts
a conversation that rises
up around
someone else's silence.
Why won't you answer me,
she hollers?

Now, there's this moment
where it seems all of nature pauses,
suspended like the sun just before
it slips through the watery horizon.
The air stills while
something dark and slippery
rolls under the dock
thumping
twice against the planks.

All over the cove
as if a signal
was given
fish start rising, snouts
dimple the surface,
nibbling at a forbidden
world, wholly
unaware of the complications
of having feet.

Hiatus

He's hungry, but not for food
so she feeds him other things instead,
like the images of the famous stones
of Pere LaChaise,
photographs she'd taken
from her other life.

He smiles, asks carefully and with
permission, smoothes the plastic back
to lightly rub his fingertips
over the films,
outlining silhouettes
like a painter applying
charcoal to canvas.

They talk quietly deep into the night
until they're done
and where there was nothing before,
now there was this.

The candle wick smoke coils in the air,
and hovers over their heads
like word bubbles in a pencil drawing.
She closes the scrapbook and ties it
with old silk ribbons and the
Mackenzie-Child seconds
get pushed away to the middle of the table,
there, at her little place on the water
where she ritually dips both feet
into her newly adopted finger lake
so far from the big sea
in Michigan where her old life waits,
a life he tried wiping up from the
photographs
to lick later on.

Opinions

I yielded the right of way to a three-car
funeral procession and followed
it for several blocks as I was
going that way anyway and

remembered something a friend
told me last night
about a fear of no one
remembering her when she
was gone or worse, about
outliving memories

and later, I knocked the headboard
three times while we made love
each whispering
into the hollow
places of coupling,
moments when
we didn't worry
our place
in anyone else's history.

because

mugg was on a
three day
whiskey and coke run
when he gave
the morning philosophy
lecture
from the corner
stool on the topic
why it is,
some men leave?

he says:
started
when they
were boys,
poorly instructed ones,
and after that
there wasn't
much
chance
of learning
what
it takes

they
don't have
words
for what
grows so big
inside
that they
disappear
from everyone
including
themselves

they
get beat
no harder
or worse than
how they beat
themselves,
regularly reminded
that they
routinely
disappoint

he pours his
bleary eyes
in with
his whiskey

maybe they
just get tired
holding up the
sky,
if they
know how,
afraid of it
falling on everyone
they love
if they don't

rheumy

is how your eyes got
at the very end,
squinting
bleary
darting
eyes
tracking
what's
ordinarily
invisible
to us,
eyes intensely
searching,
rolling
around
in their
sockets,
homing
in,
yet
no longer seeing
what we see,
instead
looking
somewhere else,
scanning
for the place
you last were
just
before
being born

norelco

shaving
my father in the hospital
was a ritual.
he managed, deciding
when and who would
shave him there
on the last bed he'd ever
lay in
dignity mostly compromised
(although he fought that)
his cathetered penis flopping out
his ass available
to the shuffling
procession of visitors

he knew he was on the way out
yet he hated leaving
fighting to stay
until the very last moment
hanging around
not to miss out
on anything
so shaving
was staying ready

it's springtime here and sun
streams through the window
falling on his face
and in that light right
at that moment, he
appeared how I remembered him
from younger years ago

he's getting the electric
shaver treatment now
holding my hand steady
while he rolls his face around
that old norelco
in the familiar pattern,
his way of letting
you love him

Bye

My father's
translucent
bluing fingers
are
tapping his
chest
near death,
he's
playing the
theme music
for the furious
dance
that was
his life

the
strumming in
morphine time
slowly slows
becomes a
requiem
misses beats
then finally
stops entirely
the conductor
ending this
rehearsal
signaling
one
final time
before
going home

DNR

The hospital social worker called,
her supervisor listening in on
another line,
asking to confirm
her end of life
instructions in the event
she becomes incapacitated
which she already has
and they repeat my words,
an echo
expressing her wishes
back from a time when
she knew what she wanted
before her mind betrayed her
and before her children gathered
to witness the end
all of us there in some fashion
around this woman,
the only one of us present
at all the beginnings

Decline

I.

She takes chicken
and ground beef
out of the freezer
every morning
to make sauce
and dresses for church,
every day a Sunday.

II.

She likes
stuffed animals now
ones that make sounds.
Her girlish giggling
reminds us that
she notices them
for the first time
every time.

III.

She moves her hands
through all the drawers
while my father sleeps
and he wakes to underwear
in the silverware drawer
so he keeps asking her
and demanding she answer:
what it is
she's looking for?

IV.

She says to me
first thing,
I had coffee with
your father this
morning. How's he
doing? I ask joining her.
Says he's doing fine
so I smile at this
fantasy, wishing it
were mine.

V.

Last night we
had a sleepover
she says
but we got in
trouble, me and
my sisters
because we got
back late. She looks
around and whispers,
they're going to
shut this place
down.
I heard
them talking
about it
with that big guy,
you know which one.

VI.

We take turns
convincing each
other that she
seems happy here
and she does
seem happy, more so
than in many years.
Maybe she just
forgot her sorrows
and this is how she
could've been
all along?

VII.

Think about
how fast things
change: one day that
next day this.
Whatever
shoves us
along into
our ordinary history
is well built and
muscular,
almost acrobatic,

so you never
really feel it
coming until
it's right there
sidling up
alongside you.

VIII.

You tell me,
how long have
I been in this
place and
where's your father?
It's not like
him not to come!
Who's watching
my house? Someone better
answer me, dammit!
Someone help me
get up! I have to get out of here,
something's burning on the stove.
What's wrong with you,
can't you smell it? AM I THE
ONLY ONE SMELLING IT!
What's wrong with all of you?
One of you
better damn well answer your mother.

Wakes

Funeral photo shows
looping in
black and white
then later,
color stills.

The predeceased
returned to life
on the flat screen
resurrected in time
for this reunion.

Image by Skeeze

Skin

From the hospital,
she says that the air
seems different now,
says its dense with
the bits and bytes
chipped from the living
who're trapped in
overlapping bandwidths
and we've become like moths
drawn to, and flicking around
that alternative rainbow
drained of colors.

She says no one can avoid it
and she presses that nothing's
like it used to be,
seems everything's
been disturbed.

She sees it everywhere:
in the birds,
one cardinal in particular,
every sunrise and sunset
it flies into the windows,
methodically working
its way around the house,
never missing a day
flinging itself at its
reflection and she sees it in
the robins that pushed their
still wet-feathered
babies out of the nest early.
Unable to fly, they hop
around on the ground.

The dog, whose
ears and nose are
always up,
bounds after them
trapping and killing until
she finally snaps a ligament
in her leg and is hobbled.

Home now and trailing whispers,
she falls asleep. The wind she hates
leaks through the floorboards and
infiltrates the mattress.
Drafts are all around her.

Later that night,
a branch snaps off
and scrapes the roof
on its way down.
Startled awake,
she jolts up in bed.
Rubbing her eyes,
she tells me through
knuckles about her
dreaming naked people
running a stampede,
their hands covering their
flopping parts, sagging
skin jiggling,
great legions of nakedness
funneling at an entryway
cut into the side of
a mountain where men
in shiny tunics wave
their arms shouting, "this way,
this way,"
and she narrates this great push
of hysterical humanity
throwing each other aside,
frantic for the door.
Many fall and are trampled,
others are crushed against
the rock. They scream.
She tells me how she hangs back,
in the dream with some others
watching the goings on from a safe distance. She's
puzzled by their indifference. They just point
she says, to the place where
someone slipped down
and disappeared beneath the horde.

Some of them laugh. There
was no end to it.
They just kept coming.

Downstairs, the dog,
her shaved, surgically
repaired leg collapsed on itself,
whines while the dream memory
slowly dissolves.

You weren't in the dream,
she tells me,
but I had a feeling you'd
left just
before I got there
and I couldn't help
thinking you
might've done something
to start that stampede.
These words ignite
her eyes and they flash quick
before going dark again.

The wind stays high
in the trees, rearranging
her memories, muddled and out of order.
Just tell me the truth, she says,
did you do something in my dream?
Did you?

The sun comes up red behind
her and lights her hair on fire.
Why did you set the dog
on those baby robins,
she says, her voice so chilling
that I flinch at the prospect of another day
spent with the reflection
of who she used to be.
Me and that cardinal, birds of a feather.

Séance

It begins
like any ordinary dream,
me dreaming up
a banquet table
of rosemary stuffed
chicken and dumplings
that suddenly jolts,
like frames from a dropped
video camera jolt and
then there's me licking
fingers
peeping thru a doorway
at thirteen ghost relatives
sitting around a table
eating tangerines
and peeled chestnuts
soaked in homemade wine,
drinking
ghost highballs.

One by one
they throw their
rubbery ghost necks at my
direction, their white eyes
cold and dead.
The chatter settles down and
they start a limp
and out of time clapping
that eventually synchronizes
into a rhythm that shakes
the chandelier so hard that
pieces of ceiling plaster
fall in their drinks.
One by one,
they levitate to dance,
bendable, wireless
marionettes flopping around,
speed clapping faster and faster
in a brightening white light
that finally flashes and pops
unbearably scalding my retina and ear.

I try to make a getaway but
they snake line follow me,
stepping over the broken bits
of ceiling and wall
and spilled drinks,
to lay siege on my house
where a couple of them
sneak in and try pulling me
off my couch down
through a basement door
down some
winding damp, stone stairs
where in a flickering
subterranean light,
I fight them, punching into their
nothingness, their lifeless
whiteness bruising
whiter, the entire sequence
showing eerie in that
impossible light and I fight
until they retreat, disintegrating
in the dawn.

I paid for a séance just to hear
what they wanted. Twenty
bucks for the madam to conjure.
She was with them when she asked:
have you ever seen them during the day?
I tell her: sometimes one or two might
glide through dark corner shadows,
causing a cold, damp wintery draft
to come up. She broke off of them,
turned on all the lights
and grabbed both my hands:
don't ever let them
see you shiver, is what she said.

Insomnia

Outside, the full moon seeps faint light
through the swollen, fast moving
charcoal night sky. Perhaps, like Galileo
you can watch the late autumn winds
move the spent season
one hemisphere over
into someone else's fall.

Finally,
the dawn creeps, showing
a soft rain falling that wet-stains
the sides of the barn, etching
a pattern to the slanting wind.

He gets up from the only chair
in this otherwise empty room
looking out on the wind cut silhouettes
seeing everything that there is to see,
clean and freshly washed as they are,
all the things he could still name.

slick

back
then
up in Joe's
older brother's room
what seems like
a hundred years ago
listening to Dylan
and Neil Young
reading Kerouac
Tolkein, man
we were
living back then
we had adventures
highjinx and escapades
fast cars, some crime

back
then
we earned
nicknames
that meant something

now
we see each other
only once in a while
in Home Depot
where we discuss
what aches us
our eyes
wondering how
we stopped being hungry
how we settled for
things we saw
our parents hating?

Query

You ever wonder
what we've become
in the years since
we played
simple games
all day running in
golden sunlight
not running away
from something
but running towards
something
something not
necessarily better
but just different
because even then
we knew
sameness
murders us
surely
like every
other killing thing?

Amends

Standing on the second story
deck off our bedroom
looking west over
the night stubbled fields
to the vast open place that's
the deepness of the lake
where the night sky lights
go to drown

It's one of the final autumn nights
and I thought I smelled
lilac even though the
bush below was long seeded
and the heavy night dew
was a single degree short of frosting

To pass time,
I pretend to chart the sky
like I pretended when I was a kid
before all of this
back when just
pretend knowledge
was all you needed
to get by

What luxury
those days of bluffing
must've been

Raymond Bizzari lives and writes in Ledyard, New York in a home built after the Revolutionary War that later became a stop on the Underground Railroad. His short stories have appeared in Lake Effect and The New Press. *Complications of Having Feet* is his first published chapbook.